HELLO!

LET'S LEARN THE

02

O
R
S
03

RED

RED

04

ORANGE

ORANGE

YELLOW
YELLOW

PINK

BLUE
BLUE

GREEN

GREEN

PURPLE

PURPLE

BLACK

TOYS

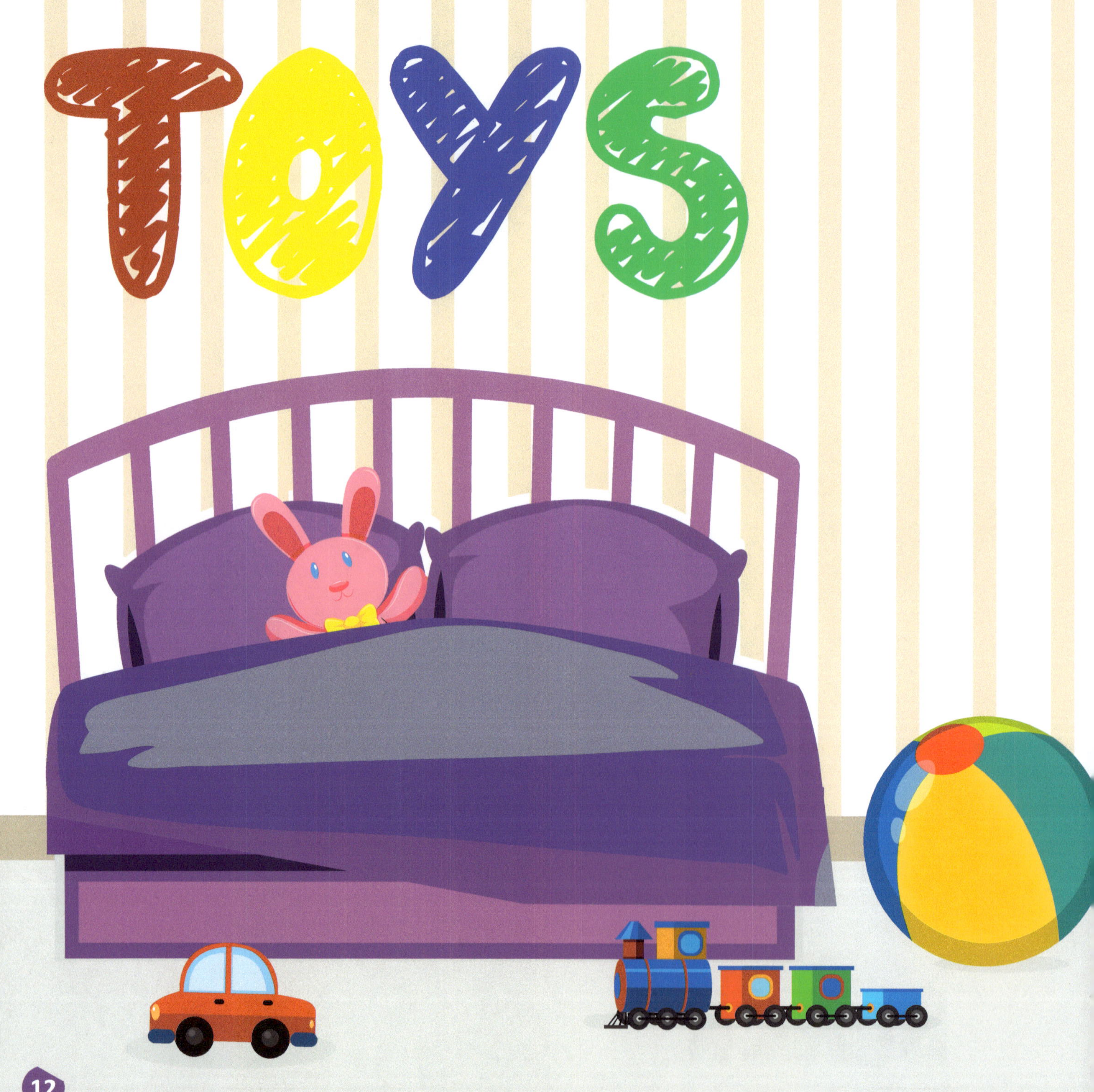

BALL

BALL

BALLOON

BALLOON

BEAR

BEAR

DOLL

DOLL

BLOCKS

BLOCKS

CAR

CAR

KITE

PUZZLE

PUZZLE

SHAPES

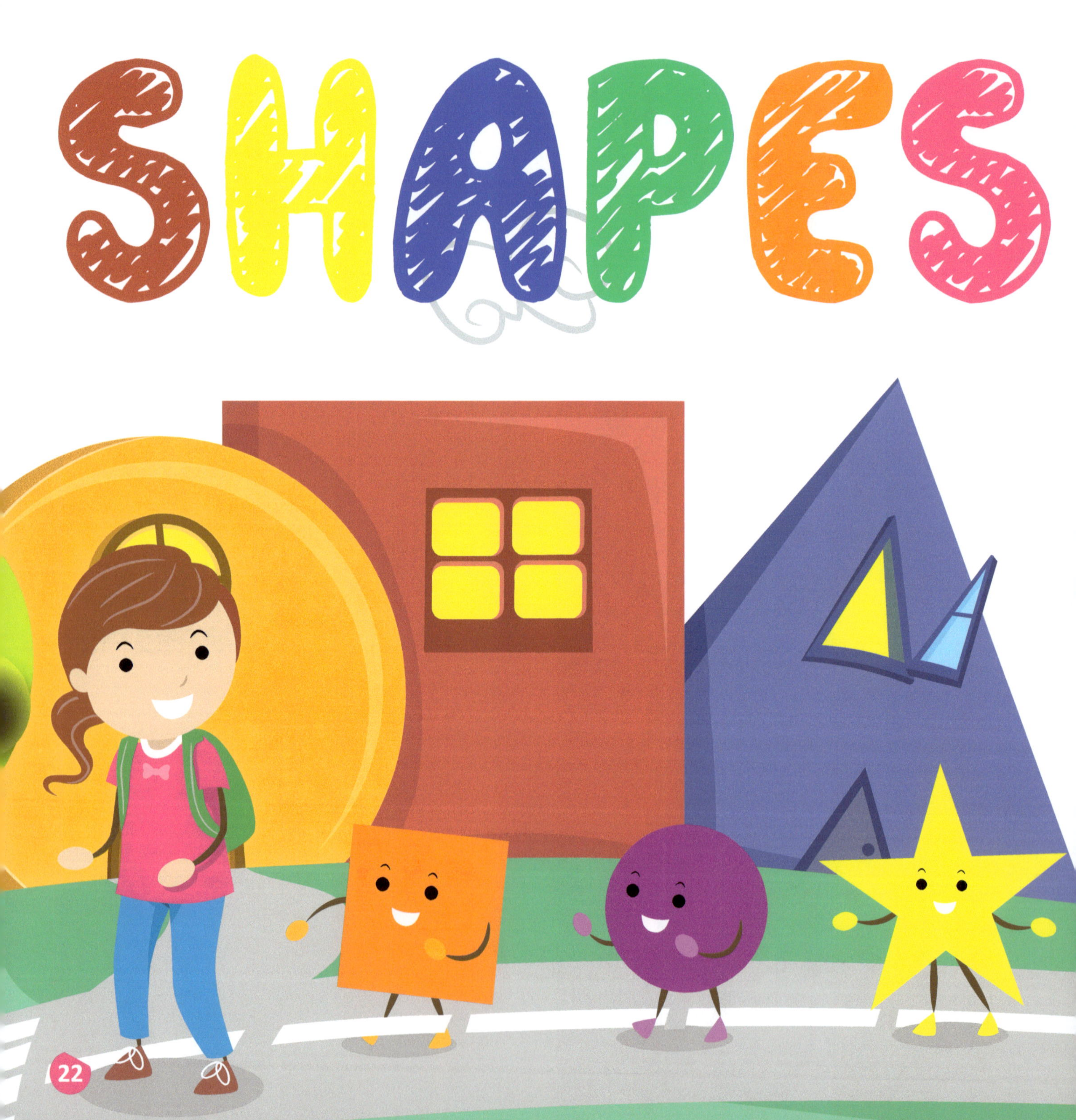

SQUARE

CIRCLE

STAR

TRIANGLE

HEART

RECTANGLE

FRUITS

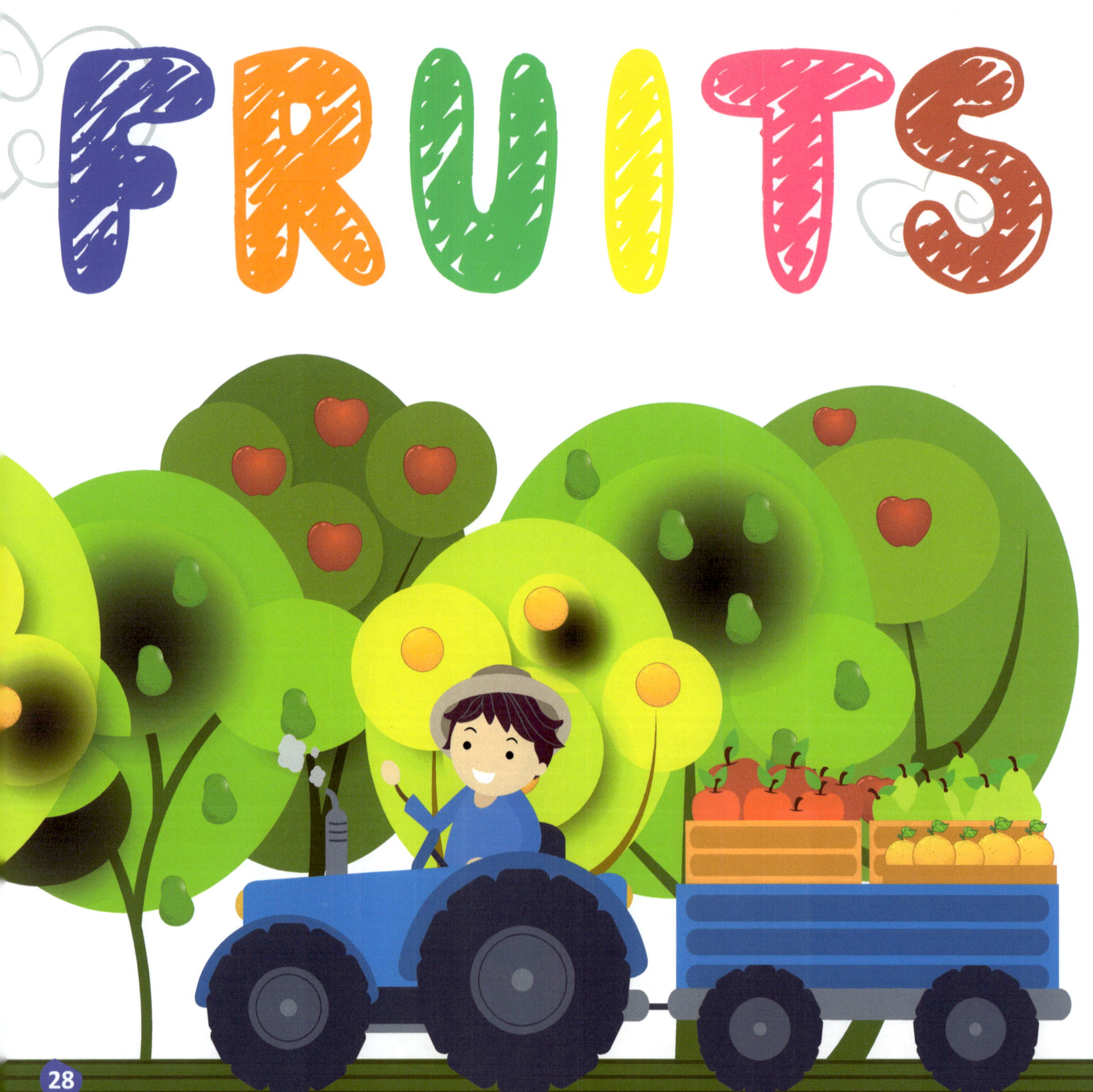

ORANGE

PEAR

BANANA

APPLE

WATERMELON

GRAPE

FOOD AND DRINKS

RICE

CRACKER

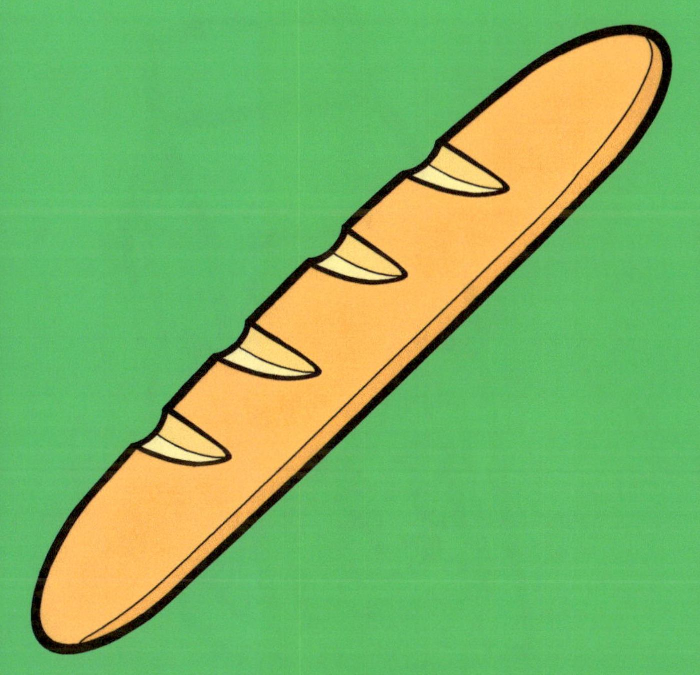

BREAD

SPAGHETTI

JUICE

MILK

YOGURT

WATER

EMOTIONS

Zzz
EMOTIONS

HAPPY

SAD

TIRED

SLEEPY

GOODBYE!